Cellulose Pajamas
Prose Poems

Meg Pokrass

BLUE LIGHT PRESS ◆ I ST WORLD PUBLISHING

1ST WORLD
PUBLISHING

SAN FRANCISCO ◆ FAIRFIELD ◆ DELHI

WINNER OF THE 2014 BLUE LIGHT BOOK AWARD

CELLULOSE PAJAMAS

Copyright ©2015 by Meg Pokrass

1ST WORLD LIBRARY
PO Box 2211
Fairfield, Iowa 52556
www.1stworldpublishing.com

BLUE LIGHT PRESS
www.bluelightpress.com
Email: bluelightpress@aol.com

BOOK & COVER DESIGN
Melanie Gendron

AUTHOR PHOTO
Miriam Berkley

FIRST EDITION

ISBN: 9781421837437

ACKNOWLEDGMENT

Grateful acknowledgement is made to the following journals in which these pieces originally appeared:

Elimae, Newport Review, Right Hand Pointing, Camroc Press Review, FRIGG, Eclectica, Everyday Genius, Up-The-Staircase, CUTTHROAT, NANO Fiction, Garygoyle, Wigleaf, Used Furniture Review, Split Lip Review

For Molly

CONTENTS

CELLULOSE PAJAMAS

I consult a nutritionist who believes in dark greens: collards, kale, chard. Hope blows in like swallows nudging the window ledge. I wash the dark green leaves carefully, softly, just for him. We will share them on the drive to the grocery store, wrap ourselves in their cool cellulose pajamas, tell each other in bird language again and again, how it was we grew too close.

SCRAPS

Ma says stand back while she strikes the match, lighting the Wedgewood stove. There is an end-of-the-world whoosh as gas and flame mate — omelets out of scraps are keen, she says sucking a Menthol — arranging button mushrooms as eyes, red onion slices into tight little smiles. At dinner, my sister's hair hangs like a thick curtain around her face. Sometimes I'll poke through it, whispering, how much for your last three bites? A dollar, she'll say. Ma can even make a piece of cooked cow look lovely, we both agree, trying to raise two children on her own. My sister excuses herself for the bathroom after dinner. Mom and I look at each other as the sink hisses, then the angry toilet joins the music.

GUEST STAR

Rain is starting. My sister stands next to her groom, and to the rabbi, exotic animal, her special guest star. The groom, hawk handsome, is shelter. Our yard is protected by a huge palm a fig tree sprouting out between its roots. Guests are cooing unanimously, as if roosting. I'm nineteen, slouching, holding a wilting bouquet. My mother and I feel light, as if drunk, as if we could lean forward forever and not fall. And in the air the good luck smell of wet grass.

Night, Monkey

Night, Monkey!" he said. Rain grabbed my window, settled as dust. My father, the world explorer, back from a mission of taking pictures, sneaking into ruins his face a crumpled map; streets, volcanoes, wind. God told me about you, I said. He laughed, told me the truth — world travelers search until they drop. His eyes sizzled like fat. I followed him anyway — to slums and secret meetings, to hear his laugh, to understand his game of secrets.

SETTLING

He took my hand, led me to the bathroom, opened the door and slipped in. The bathroom was dark. Through the partially opened window, an apartment with a yellow breakfast nook. His breath was on my mouth with the smell of fruit and white wine, sweet and sour sauce. This was where he felt safest; bathrooms, closets, tiny, ridiculous places.

Earlier that night, at a movie, I'd listened to him eating un-buttered popcorn. How each piece squeaked in his teeth. I believed I'd grow to hate this sound, and the idea made me want to plant my hand on his knee, which I did.

There were many ways to love, and to be loved, and none of them were just the way you dreamed as a child. My mother had been relieved to lounge around in an old, stained bathrobe, watch the news and fall asleep after my father left. Some people don't want the worries of entanglement, Mom had said. Some people prefer the music of their own lives.

Siren

"There is a flustered buffalo in a hotel bed, and it is a man, and it is a man who wants me so much he is levitating like an endangered animal. He is mastering the art of being made extinct. I am that kind of pony, here today, gone tomorrow, all fancy and prancing and cruel. I administer pleasure, and then disappear, because I can, because I am a splinter, that is all I am when not making an animal happy.

There are the ones to take inside and to rock like babies, to rock until they groan and ask for pancakes.

There are ways to fly up against the heat of a man's sex, to singe his wings because nothing lasts longer than a good beer, or a fingerling potato on a cold night.

Emerald

He asked her to choose a shade of green. He liked the way she stooped to tie her shoes like an old man, as though she could fall over very easily.

Go! he said.

The window was open and she screamed it. He asked again.

BIG SISTER

The night my first period started my sister and I were watching the movie Harvey and we laughed.

Her hair seemed heavy on her shoulders, a long, thick curtain.

I peered through whenever I could to catch a glimpse of her strong cheek bones moving.

Later that night she told me about an adventure she had with a man until I fell asleep.

When I woke up, I snuck into the living room, and found her there talking to the cat.

The cat was laughing.

TOLL FREE KALE

During the day, my husband snores in rhythm with the dog. Some may say it is cute. I would not say that exactly. Today, two or three beautiful women on Facebook offer me favors. One offers me something I'm too embarrassed to speak about, and another offers virtual grapes. Dennis offers to leave Facebook and does. There is something wrong with my home phone — the landline. It rings, and the caller ID says "Toll free kale." I knew Dennis was gay from day one. It is difficult for women like myself to accept certain things about the world's Dennises because they are perfect for us. Another vague come-on from a Facebook friend goes like this: I am a very straight man, but a lesbian in my soul . . ." I'm sure some men are, inside their souls, lesbians. Yet, if I wanted a woman, I would find a woman. Also, I am married. My husband is sleeping right next to my computer. The dog and he.

Baking

Gathering in the living room for wine on Christmas Eve — coughing, moving chairs at commercials. I would have started baking three days ago, mom says, in a monotone. At the stove, I'm already scorching the second batch, remembering the tune Rick made up, the way he whistled it naked. Cookie sheet's warped; sifter's missing a handle. Puppy trips mom near the bathroom.

Jesus, she hoots.

I drive to 7-11 to buy more flour, puppy in my lap. On his cell Jay says his manic brother showed up — spun a web in the corner of the living room. His mother's crying and drinking after a year dry.

Merry Christmas, I say.

He tells me we should get married, move to Mexico, become Buddhists.

Buddhists, I say, inhaling puppy's breath in the cold car, snow falling like rice.

LAST CAUSE

Tonight I ate crackers with guilt instead of cheese, thought about my cousin who is round as weeble. I see gum on the sidewalk, ignore it, I know assholes and he is not one. He is tender, tucks it under his umbrella, his mind can taste it. Let's say there is no successful love poem. I compare this to a strike of the heart toward the very last cause, maybe the only bird born that round and soft, so much beauty that nobody knows what the fuck to call it, what kind of bird it is.

MAP

His face was my landscape, before it went dark, I found him outside alone; brushing lint off his shirt, out there in the invisible city night gazing up at his sky.

Ruby

I nibble popcorn while the movie burns through my body. I'm his Ruby Throated hummingbird, fighting to be still though quivery when he says it, he says *Suck the popcorn, my girl, take time with it in your mouth, each salty buttery piece as I will you, and I will let you fly.*

SALTY

It was when she loved a man with eyes like a fishbowl everything changed. With his kisses she would swallow clear water. Fear would rest behind colored pebbles, be gone for entire seconds — long enough to bubble inside and out. I love this, she spit, swallowing his air, his name, dancing backwards with it in her lips.

Primping

In the photo he looks ragged, fierce, wears a bandana. He lives with his father, up north. I am thirteen, rushing from mirror to mirror, removing childhood by applying blue eye-shadow, black eyeliner. I stare for half an hour at the perfect rings around my eyes.

Mom is out selling houses. I am alone, baking cookies, imagining him on a beach. I sculpt the raw dough and roll it out, just right.

DIVE

My sister says nothing, though to me the place is new and marvelous. When I shut the front door I hear her singing.

The air outside in the high sun like a blow dryer. Out by the pool a root beer-skinned boy looks me over as though I dropped from a tree. A group of girls near him squawk about something they *absolutely agree on.*

I watch while he dives for them into the aquamarine pool, his fingers carving the first slice.

Nurse

The fourth month, one of her tricks was being his nurse. She'd bring a towel and put it on his forehead. She noticed he preferred pencils to pens, made shopping lists, *Please, please buy these things!* the lists would say at the very top. Q-tips for paint brushes. Homemade paint from coffee grounds. He painted birds, mainly. *Honey,* she'd say, *this is better than anything.*

Please, she said, *teach me.*

CLIMBING OUT

I wake at dawn when he bangs his mini-gong. His mouth wide, lips so flexible they could swallow a rabbit. I'm afraid to jinx anything, climbing out of his futon. "Talk is breaking many rules, but listening is holy," he said last night when he sawed me in half but didn't. I listen to him listening. The city smells salty, orange light sneaks around his shower-curtained window, cabs call like geese, or mothers of missing children.

Singing

He didn't allow my mother to sing, but once she tried, with me on her lap.

I remember the forbidden sound of her voice, the way it trembled like snow on the tips of my ears.

She thought he was relaxing, taking an herb bath. He was a doctor, and needed his sanity.

He ran out of the bathroom yelling *stop singing*! smelling just like the holidays.

SENTRY

No windows; but somehow the spiders got in. Dozens, every day, along with smells of salmon oil, coffee grounds, mold. One morning he was snoring off red wine, a long fight, when a shadow scampered over his stomach. She froze — couldn't kill it, woke him up before anything else happened. She lived alone with the spiders all day while he worked. Before he came back, she'd check the single futon throwing the covers off, just standing — watching.

To-Do List

Wake adolescent with softest mom voice, tell her it's time to get up and ready for school. She hates to be ten-seconds late, because she hates to be noticed. Cut puzzle pieces of parboiled meat for sick cat, microwave low, re-animate, sprinkle cat vitamins. Measure out dog food, mix with pumpkin and green beans for dog diet. Isolate other cat in bathroom with stars of kibble. Apply lipstick, deflate hair with water — forgive it. Prepare for drive to school by finding keys in purse despite napkins, planet stickers, half-eaten food bars. Talk to dog about losing things all the time. Unwrap and reassemble self.

Alarm

My boyfriend is acting like fireflies I caught and jarred as a child, though he hasn't lost his flashing, gold eyes. Sometimes he seems almost happy to be with me — laying on his floor mat stretching, moving a brown leg up and down slowly, readying to fly.

Dr. V.

My foot is darker than the ocean. It's turning blue — He promises to stop the pain and I picture him in a world of shark eggs, he rolls them toward me like unbreakable promises and there is nothing to do but keep them. When he calls he sounds tired, blue gauze covers his telephone voice. I want to soothe him, but that's not my role. Twitching fish, bones and blue cartilage, I can't help shivering, picturing his needle between my toes.

WIDOWER

She sleeps at his apartment once a month, and warms his hands between her thighs. Her open, shell-shaped mouth kisses his closed lips. Her tongue, only once, tried to pry them open.

"Otter," he calls her, knotting her hair with his knuckles.

An otter is just an otter.

People say he howled for months after his wife drowned. Then, he went and rescued incurable, difficult dogs. The neighbors were embarrassed by the whole thing; the limping dogs, the howling.

Viewing

The black cat's *Rowel? Rowel?* woke me, plum tree branches ratted the window as if trying to get in, my husband breathed evenly near the wall. 4AM was too early for the last baby feeding, late enough to remember who we were before the baby. Out of bed, nearly tripped over the sick cat yowling for water. *We're all in trouble! Now, shush! don't wake baby!*

The New

In the morning when she opened one eye, his face was above hers. *You look like a turtle*, he said.

Half asleep she felt a surrounding shell. In her dream about him he was a spotted owl, peering around the meadow ready to choose which mouse had caused the trouble.

Turtle, he whispered, stroking her hair . . .

Kissing her awake.

RECOGNITION

My mother is afraid and forgetful. When a person is mourning they don't know they are. The best dog should find you, they say, but will it? Inside your neck a man waits to kiss you and maybe a cat sits all day in your little house. Your kid says you are too permissive, and she is taller than you now. When you first met him, there was no recognition. There are kids in the military, and that is why they'll caress a gun, amazed they will die. The moon is chicken-soup yellow.

KNOT

His eyes were green, the rest of his face falling. It was morning again, a planet of mornings. That's why he placed dishes so carefully on the edge, he was broken before slipping.

Someone walked in and said hello. I ordered a Cappuccino. A man smiled and looked at the chairs.

I felt the knot in my voice, *hello, hi hi,* I was only talking to tell us both we were there.

PEAS AND CHEESE

She wakes up loving him but not hard enough. He has dandelion hair. Stars fall and zip between them, they can't stop laughing; she falls asleep curled around him like a comma. He is gay, and often, he reminds her that she deserves better. She nods seriously and then forgets. She suggests dinner. Peas with melted cheese. He lets her do that for him.

Fertile

She was doing a summer walk with her dog. Restaurants were full, fertile green salads everywhere. Men sat with women and kissed them. Birds flew overhead and made insanely pretty sounds.

African Butterfly

You're two hundred miles farther from father now, and you know it is good, but you could open the door and jump right on a train and go back. Not many kids would but you could. You excel at stunts.

When you step out onto the porch the mosquito screen reminds you that you're an African butterfly, right before the first white stars.

Knock

She asked him when the knock would come and he said, "Anytime you live in a cottage it is imminent, the knock is so ready to happen, they tend to come about in the winter."

The knock she pictured was loose, and would put her into a trance of cloudy, jazzy sounds, she may follow the knock all the way to the next cottage, so in some way she hoped a knock would not happen. She didn't want to leave him. So they both waited.

HE

Twenty years later and sometimes, beside my daughter, stands
a different child — as though he were listening to our days. It
feels as though he would have been a HE — this hungry child who
comes often and quietly just to be with us, and never feels full, or
figures out exactly what we may have said.

EMPTY

Nobody will have that me again.

When you had me and I had you and we watched movies eating popcorn with brewer's yeast, holding fingers, just fingers.

So sit down.

Just sit there.

Tell me without your eyes, because fuck them, they do not let me in—those people were snapshots created to please each other, and you are talking with your mouth full, so fast and empty in here, and quiet.

I remember.

VAULT OF GREAT THINGS

The way she remembers it, her father planted strawberry trees. That is what she stashes in the vault of great things he did. She imagines a yard of them — reddish trees with curly limbs. Her sisters and she picking strawberries, secure with a myth that children are happy.

About the Author

Meg Pokrass is the author of "Damn Sure Right" (Press 53, 2011); "My Very End of the Universe, Five Mini-Novellas-in-Flash and a Study of the Form" (Rose Metal Press, 2014) and "Bird Envy" (Harvard Bookstore bestseller). Her stories have appeared in more than 200 literary magazines and anthologies, including *McSweeney's Internet Tendency, PANK, Green Mountains Review, Five Points,* and numerous anthologies, including *Flash Fiction International* (W.W. Norton). A third full flash fiction collection "The Dog Looks Happy Upside Down" is forthcoming from Etruscan Press (Spring, 2016). Meg serves as associate editor for Frederick Barthelme's *New World Writing*, and is the founder of *New Flash Fiction Review*. Meg currently divides her time between San Francisco and London, England.

Printed in the United States of America